Growth, Distribution, and Poverty in Africa

MESSAGES FROM THE 1990s

POVERTY DYNAMICS IN AFRICA

POVERTY DYNAMICS IN AFRICA SERIES

This volume is one of a series of studies completed under the Poverty Dynamics in Africa Initiative, which is organized by the Africa Region of the World Bank. This initiative has received support from several bilateral donors: Italy, the Netherlands, Switzerland, the United Kingdom, and the United States. The motive for the series, launched in 2002, was to make use of the vastly improved household survey data in Africa and to enhance understanding of poverty trends on this continent during the 1990s. The goal is to provide a more secure empirical basis on which to assess past progress in poverty reduction in Africa and to frame more effective policies for the future.

The countries selected for investigation are those in which the household survey data are robust and can sustain comparisons over time. Many of the studies focus on income (or consumption) poverty and seek to link poverty outcomes to wider economic change, including economic policy reforms, in the countries concerned. Other studies use demographic and health surveys, which have provided invaluable information about the well-being of African people—especially the children. Further information can be obtained from Poverty Reduction and Economic Management (PREM) in the Africa Region of the World Bank.

Growth, Distribution, and Poverty in Africa

MESSAGES FROM THE 1990s

POVERTY DYNAMICS IN AFRICA

Luc Christiaensen
Lionel Demery
Stefano Paternostro

THE WORLD BANK
Washington, D.C.

Cover design: Naylor Design, Inc., Washington, DC
Cover photo credit: © Victor Englebert; Adukrom village, near Kumasi, Ghana; 1996.

ISBN 0-8213-5213-X

Library of Congress Cataloging-in-Publication Data

Christiaensen, Luc J.
    Growth, distribution, and poverty in Africa : messages from the 1990s / Luc
  Christiaensen, Lionel Demery, Stefano Paternostro.
      p. cm. — (Poverty dynamics in Africa)
    Includes bibliographical references.
    ISBN 0-8213-5213-X
     1. Poverty—Africa. 2. Income—Africa. 3. Cost and standard of living—Africa.
    4. Africa—Economic conditions—1960– 5. African—Economic policy. I. Demery,
  Lionel. II. Paternostro, Stefano. III. Title. IV. Series.

HG3881.5.W57 2002
339.2'2'096—dc21

                                       2002034960

Contents

FIGURES

Acknowledgments

This book synthesizes and builds on the work of a large team of researchers who completed a series of country studies under the Poverty Dynamics in Africa Initiative, coordinated by the Africa Region of the World Bank. It benefits enormously from their careful and competent analysis. The authors are grateful for helpful comments from Alan Gelb, John Hoddinott, and Jean-Louis Arcand, and they especially acknowledge the responsive and enthusiastic research assistance of Angelica Salvi. The work was generously supported by a group of bilateral donors: Italy, the Netherlands, Switzerland, the United Kingdom, and the United States.

Abbreviations and Acronyms

CPI	Consumer price index
GDP	Gross domestic product
ICRG	International Country Risk Guide
IFAD	International Fund for Agricultural Development
PPP	Purchasing power parity

Abstract

This book reviews recent evidence on the trends in household well-being in Africa during the 1990s. It draws on the findings of a series of studies on poverty dynamics that use the better data sets now available. It begins by taking a broad view of poverty, tracing changes in both income poverty and other, more direct measures of individual welfare. Experiences have been varied: some countries have seen sharp decreases in income poverty, whereas others have witnessed marked increases. Economic growth has in the aggregate been pro-poor, but the aggregate numbers hide significant and systematic distributional effects that have caused some groups to be left behind.

This volume draws four key conclusions. First, economic policy reforms (improving macroeconomic balances and liberalizing markets) have been conducive to reductions in poverty. Second, location matters for poverty reduction strategies in Africa. Some regions, by virtue of their sheer remoteness, have been left behind when growth has picked up. The role of infrastructure (especially access to roads) is crucial. Third, education and access to land are key private endowments to help households benefit from emerging economic opportunities and to enable them to escape poverty. Finally, the evidence reviewed here underscores the significance of social protection in a poverty reduction strategy. Ill health and the impact of rainfall variations are the risk factors featured as having profound effects on poverty outcomes in Africa.

Introduction

oes the Dollar and Kraay (2000, p. 27) view—that "anyone who cares about the poor should favor the growth-enhancing policies of good rule of law, fiscal discipline, and openness to international trade"—apply to Africa in the 1990s? Or was the growth path the reforms induced characterized by increasing inequality, which denied benefits to the poorest (Forsyth 2000; Mkandawire and Soludo 1999; Stewart 1995)? There is no simple answer to this question, given the many changes that affected people's lives and livelihoods in Africa during the 1990s. In addition to economic and political reforms, external opportunities and constraints shifted during the decade, with many countries experiencing sharp movements in their terms of trade. Some countries faced internal civil strife and political instability. Others had to endure severe droughts. And there have been serious health shocks, such as AIDS (acquired immunodeficiency syndrome) and malaria, that have affected rich and poor alike. The effects of these changes on growth and poverty were further conditioned by the private and public endowments households possessed—their physical assets, their human capital, and their access to infrastructure and public services. This complexity makes for considerable debate about the relationship between policy, growth, and poverty in Africa—a debate that was previously not always well served with hard evidence.

It is by now widely accepted that economic growth is at least a necessary condition for sustainable poverty reduction (Kanbur 2001). Yet historically, growth rates have been low in Africa. In a review of the literature of cross-country growth studies, Collier and Gunning (1999) conclude that the explanations for this phenomenon are to be found in geographical circumstances, for example, the land-locked, tropical character of many countries; in macroeconomic policies, notably economic policy volatility and a lack of openness to international trade; and in microeconomic policies, which have disproportionately taxed rural producers, eroded social capital, undermined the provision of public services, and resulted in a retreat into subsistence by rural producers.

Despite these important insights from cross-country analysis, the reasons for "Africa's growth and poverty paradox" (Easterly and Levine 1997) remain much debated. The limited number of countries and the high correlation between the explanatory variables mean that the findings are often highly sensitive to the specification of the estimation model. Cross-country studies typically examine average long-term growth and are therefore unable to deal with some of the important growth dynamic issues, such as the deterioration in African growth after the 1960s and the tendency for growth in Africa to be episodic in nature (Collier and Gunning 1999). The use of countrywide averages in this literature also limits what can be said about the distributional dimension of growth, particularly its relation to poverty. And the fact that the cross-country evidence often emphasizes immutable factors, such as geography and linguistic or ethnic fragmentation, limits its relevance to policy formulation in any particular country.

The messages from household-level analyses are different from those of the cross-country literature. Among the factors explaining poverty at the household level, "disease and climate feature most prominently, and these are largely omitted in the aggregate analysis" (Collier and Gunning 1999, p. 83). They hint that these growth-retarding risks may explain the "Africa dummy" in growth regressions.[1] Also, the lack of credit appears more constraining to rural households than would be suggested by the aggregate growth models. It is unlikely that cross-country analysis alone will resolve the growth–poverty issue (Bourguignon 2000; Brock and Durlauf 2000; Deininger and Okidi 2001).

Ravallion (2001) also calls for a more microeconomic approach to the analysis of policies, growth, and poverty. Using household survey data in a sample of 50 developing countries and 120 spells of poverty change, he estimates that on average the growth elasticity of headcount poverty is –2.5.[2,3] That average, however, masks a great deal of variation across countries— variations related to the level and trends in income inequality. Inequality impinges on the growth–poverty relationship in three ways. First, high initial inequality can harm subsequent growth, although the body of evidence on this is somewhat mixed.[4] Second, high initial inequality undermines the poverty-reducing potential of growth. This is because even when income distributions remain unchanged, poor groups gain from overall growth roughly in proportion to their initial share in the national pie. The higher the initial inequality, the lower the share of the poor, and the less poverty reduction is generated by a growth in mean income.[5] Third, *changes* in inequality will modify the poverty-reducing effects of mean income growth. Among the countries experiencing increasing living standards in his sample, Ravallion finds that the annual reduction in poverty was only 1.3 percent in countries where inequality was rising—compared with 9.6 percent in the countries experiencing falling inequality. He concludes the following:

> These observations point to the importance of more micro, country-specific, research on the factors determining why some poor people are able to take up the opportunities afforded by an expanding economy—and so add to its expansion—while others are not. Individual endowments of physical and human capital have rightly been emphasized in past work, and they suggest important links to policy. Other factors that may well be equally important have received less attention, such as location, social exclusion and exposure to uninsured risk. (p. 1813)

This book applies this advice to Africa by using the much-improved data base in the region. It addresses three central questions:

a. What does recent household survey evidence tell us about the evolution of overall poverty and inequality in Africa and their relationship to economic growth (and stagnation)?
b. Moving beyond the national averages, did particular population groups or geographical regions gain or lose from the episodes of reform-induced growth?

c. Among the wide array of disparate events and factors affecting growth and poverty trends, which emerge as key in explaining changes in income distribution and poverty?

This volume builds on the results of a series of country studies completed under the Poverty Dynamics in Africa Initiative that exploit household survey data in Africa covering the 1990s.[6] It examines the main factors behind observed poverty trends by first taking a *macro perspective*, linking the historical changes in income poverty in our sample countries to changes in economic environment—the macroeconomic and sectoral policy frameworks, and the institutional settings. It then exploits the survey data to greater depth by taking a *micro perspective*. This assesses the way households—poor households in particular—have been affected by the events of the 1990s and distinguishes between the effects of policies and of shocks. When available, household panel data have been used (Ethiopia and Uganda), although important insights were also obtained from repeated cross-sections (Ghana, Madagascar, and Zimbabwe). The text highlights the main insights emerging from this sample of micro-econometric country studies in Africa.

Considering that well-being is multifaceted, this book begins with a review of the changes that have occurred in income, education, nutrition, and health. Chapter 1 first examines how these four different dimensions of well-being have evolved during the 1990s at the aggregate level. It then moves beyond the aggregates and examines their evolution across income quintiles, focusing particularly on how welfare of the poorest groups fared. The chapter concludes by describing the evolution of overall income poverty and inequality, and its relationship to economic growth. The two subsequent chapters seek to explain the systematic changes in income distribution and poverty in Africa, taking both macro (chapter 2) and micro (chapter 3) perspectives. Concluding observations are made in the final chapter.

CHAPTER 1

Living Standards during the 1990s

To set the scene, table 1 reports four basic measures of well-being: private consumption, primary school enrollment, child malnutrition, and child mortality. The first and obvious point to note is that living standards are very low in these countries. By the close of the decade, no country enjoyed an annual per capita consumption in excess of US$500, and in Ethiopia it was just US$86. All countries fall far short of universal primary school enrollment, and in some (for example, Ethiopia) primary enrollments are unacceptably low. Malnutrition is also a very serious problem, especially in Ethiopia and Madagascar. In Ethiopia, about two-thirds of children exhibit signs of stunting or long-term malnutrition (defined as the percentage of children with low height for age compared with a reference population). Even in Ghana, Mauritania, and Zimbabwe, there is evidence of stunting in about a quarter of the population under five years of age. Perhaps the most poignant indicator of the very low welfare levels of these countries is the incidence of child deaths. Under-age-five mortality exceeds 100 (per 1,000) in all countries. In Zambia, almost one in five children fail to survive to their fifth birthday. Too many African children are dying needlessly.

Second, there are differences in the *changes* in these indicators over time. In four countries economic living standards appear to have improved. In Madagascar, however, average real consumption remained more or less unchanged, whereas it fell sharply in Nigeria, Zambia, and

Table 1. Evolving Living Standards in Eight African Countries during the 1990s

Country and survey years	Real private consumption per capita (constant 1995 US$)[a]			Net primary school enrollment rates[b]			Child malnutrition[c]			Child mortality[d]		
	Year 1	Year 2	Annual growth rate (%)	Year 1 (%)	Year 2 (%)	Change (% points)	Year 1 (%)	Year 2 (%)	Change (% points)	Year 1 (per 1,000)	Year 2 (per 1,000)	Change (per 1,000)
Positive growth												
Ethiopia 1994–97	80	86	2.6	19	25	+6	66	55	–11	190	175	–15
Ghana 1992–98	275	304	2.0	70	82	+12	26	26	0	119	104	–15
Mauritania 1987–95	297	361	3.6	28	41	+13	48	23	–25	—	149	—
Uganda 1992–97	211	258	4.7	68	86	+18	43	39	–4	165	162	–3
Stagnation or decline												
Madagascar 1993–99	223	222	0.0	48	64	+16	50	49	–1	170	149	–21
Nigeria 1992–96	206	173	–3.4	94	98	+4	38	—	—	136	147	11
Zambia 1991–98	362	266	–6.6	73	66	–7	40	42	+2	194	189	–5
Zimbabwe 1991–96	595	439	–5.2	83	86	+3	30	23	–7	77	108	31

— Not available.

a. Growth rates calculated based on least squares method, which is less sensitive to the choice of base and terminal period.

b. Net enrollment rates represent the percentage of children of school age enrolled in primary school as a fraction of the total number of children in that age group. Figures obtained from the surveys analyzed in the Poverty Dynamics studies. First-year figures for Ethiopia refer to 1994 and 1996 and are obtained from *World Development Indicators*.

c. Child malnutrition is defined as the percentage of children stunted, that is, z-score of height for age that is less than –2; the reference periods for these figures are approximate to those in column 1.

d. Child mortality under age five (per 1,000 live births). The reference periods are approximate to those in column 1.

Source: World Bank data and country studies completed under the Poverty Dynamics in Africa Initiative (see bibliography).

Zimbabwe. Similarly, improvements in primary school enrollment in Ethiopia, Ghana, Mauritania, and Uganda contrast with unsatisfactory outcomes in Zambia. Ethiopia and Mauritania experienced sharp reductions in long-term malnutrition, but there was little progress elsewhere. In all countries the long-term downward trend in child mortality appears to have continued through the decade, except in Zimbabwe, a result probably related to the AIDS epidemic (among other factors), and in Nigeria. Also the 2000/1 round of the Uganda Demographic and Health Survey suggests that child mortality in Uganda has been unchanged (and possibly even increased) since 1995 (UDHS 2001).

Third, the trends in the indicators are generally consistent with each other, although some important exceptions exist. In the four countries experiencing economic growth (Ethiopia, Ghana, Mauritania, and Uganda), the trends in human development indicators match the improvement in economic well-being, albeit in different degrees. In those experiencing stagnation and decline, however, the signals are noisier. In some cases the education indicator improved despite the stagnation or decline in economic living standards (Madagascar, Nigeria, and Zimbabwe). Child mortality improved in Zambia, and child malnutrition improved in Zimbabwe during episodes of deteriorating economic circumstance. Such outcomes (and the experience of Uganda after 1995) serve as a reminder that focusing on only one dimension of well-being can be misleading when tracking poverty dynamics over time (World Bank 2000).

INEQUALITY IN HUMAN DEVELOPMENT

The indicators in table 1 are averages for the population as a whole. We now review the *distribution* of these indicators across the populations, identifying especially changes in the welfare of poorer households. We begin with the human development indicators. Primary school enrollments are particularly low in Ethiopia (table 2), and to a lesser extent in Mauritania. The poorest households in these countries typically do not enroll their children in primary schools. There have been major strides, however, in raising primary enrollments during the decade in Ghana, Madagascar, Mauritania, and Uganda. And where there have been educa-

Table 2. Primary School Net Enrollment Rates by Consumption Quintile for Seven African Countries (percent)

Consumption quintile	Ethiopia		Ghana		Madagascar		Mauritania		Uganda		Zambia		Zimbabwe	
	1996	1997	1992	1998	1993	1999	1987	1995	1992	1997	1991	1998	1991	1996
Poorest quintile	15	17	54	70	29	53	19	25	54	80	57	50	78	81
Second quintile	15	24	69	81	43	65	25	41	63	87	67	62	82	85
Third quintile	18	27	73	86	59	64	29	49	69	88	75	69	84	87
Fourth quintile	21	28	77	87	60	68	32	50	75	87	82	75	86	89
Richest quintile	30	33	87	90	60	78	50	60	86	89	86	81	89	91
Ratio Q1:Q5	0.50	0.52	0.62	0.78	0.49	0.68	0.47	0.42	0.63	0.89	0.67	0.62	0.88	0.89

Note: Data were provided from surveys in the years listed.
Source: Country studies completed under the Poverty Dynamics in Africa Initiative (see bibliography).

tion enrollment gains, they have included the poor. Only Zambia seems to have lost ground.

Because income data were not collected in the Demographic and Health Surveys, Sahn, Stifel, and Younger (1999) and Sahn and Stifel (2000b) constructed a proxy index for income based on assets and household amenities. This enabled them to examine trends in child health capabilities (survival and nutrition) by wealth class. The poorest 20 percent of the populations appear to be those most affected by the deterioration in preschool child nutrition (table 3). Stunting (measured by height for age) has deteriorated among the poorest in three countries (Ghana, Senegal, and Tanzania) and improved in four (Madagascar, Uganda, Zambia, and Zimbabwe). Short-term malnutrition, or wasting (measured by weight for height), however, has increased among the poorest quintiles of five countries (Ghana, Madagascar, Senegal, Uganda, and Zimbabwe). In general, these data indicate a major problem of increased wasting during the 1990s, including among the poor. This is not fully understood and clearly calls for further investigation.

Most countries have experienced declines in mortality among the poor, the exceptions being Kenya and Zambia (table 4). The trends are not always uniform across wealth groups. The ratio of mortality levels among the poorest to the richest quintiles has increased in most cases— where mortality has been falling, it has fallen faster among the richest group. The exceptions are Zambia and Zimbabwe.

INCOME INEQUALITY

We turn now to income distribution and to the issue of whether episodes of growth in the 1990s in Africa were associated with changes in income inequality. Increasing reliance on markets and the withdrawal of the state might be expected to increase income inequality (people with low levels of education and with limited access to public services and markets being less likely to take advantage of the opportunities growth presents). Conversely, the previous tendency for the state to tax agriculture and the rural sector heavily, and the removal of such state intervention, might result in improved national income distributions.

Table 3. Malnutrition by Wealth Quintile for Seven African Countries (percent)

Wealth quintile	Country and survey years													
	Ghana		Madagascar		Senegal		Tanzania		Uganda		Zambia		Zimbabwe	
	1988	1993	1992	1997	1986	1992	1991	1996	1988	1995	1992	1997	1988	1994
Height for age														
Poorest quintile	34	38	53	50	27	35	43	46	48	43	49	46	41	23
Second quintile	33	30	45	40	23	30	44	44	45	40	45	49	37	24
Third quintile	30	29	51	51	24	30	43	42	44	40	39	43	27	25
Fourth quintile	27	23	50	49	25	20	40	39	42	33	30	33	25	22
Richest quintile	21	17	44	46	13	14	26	28	27	25	27	27	12	12
Ratio Q1:Q5	1.6	2.2	1.2	1.1	2.1	2.5	1.7	1.6	1.8	1.7	1.8	1.7	3.4	1.9
Weight for height														
Poorest quintile	7	16	6	10	7	15	9	8	2	6	7	5	1	5
Second quintile	9	10	8	7	4	14	7	10	4	7	7	7	2	4
Third quintile	8	15	7	7	7	12	5	9	4	7	5	6	1	5
Fourth quintile	8	10	4	5	8	12	6	9	0	4	6	5	1	6
Richest quintile	7	9	4	5	4	8	7	6	0	4	6	4	1	5
Ratio Q1:Q5	1.0	1.8	1.5	2.0	1.8	1.9	1.3	1.3	—	1.5	1.2	1.3	1.0	1.0

Note: Percentages are for children between 3 and 36 months of age with anthropometric z-score less than −2. Data were provided from Demographic and Health Surveys in the years listed.
Source: Sahn, Stifel, and Younger 1999.

Table 4. Infant and Under-Age-Three Mortality by Asset Index for Nine African Countries

Asset index	Country and survey years										
	Ghana		Kenya		Madagascar		Mali		Senegal		
	1988	1993	1988	1993	1992	1997	1987	1995	1986	1992	1997
Infant mortality											
Poorest quintile	120	90	78	90	121	128	173	157	114	96	101
Third quintile	92	85	76	56	109	103	168	156	96	76	70
Richest quintile	74	48	55	45	88	73	102	98	81	38	47
Ratio Q1:Q5	1.6	1.9	1.4	2	1.4	1.8	1.7	1.6	1.4	2.5	2.1
Under-age-three mortality											
Poorest quintile	160	152	93	128	200	191	318	266	224	169	157
Third quintile	138	108	83	67	176	166	237	256	175	136	120
Richest quintile	113	80	60	54	135	85	184	148	114	60	66
Ratio Q1:Q5	1.4	1.9	1.6	2.4	1.5	2.2	1.7	1.8	2.0	2.8	2.4

(Table continues on the following page.)

Table 4. (continued)

Asset index	Country and survey year							
	Tanzania		Uganda		Zambia		Zimbabwe	
	1991	1996	1988	1995	1992	1997	1988	1994
Infant mortality								
Poorest quintile	114	116	141	107	134	143	66	57
Third quintile	97	89	115	100	129	101	69	54
Richest quintile	76	66	103	73	72	103	37	39
Ratio Q1:Q5	1.5	1.8	1.4	1.5	1.9	1.4	1.8	1.5
Under-age-three mortality								
Poorest quintile	156	144	189	182	217	224	84	71
Third quintile	152	138	184	168	187	184	92	70
Richest quintile	127	91	158	100	103	147	36	53
Ratio Q1:Q5	1.2	1.6	1.2	1.8	2.1	1.5	2.3	1.3

Note: Data given for five-year cohorts of children born one and three years prior to the survey, respectively, per 1,000 births. Data were provided from Demographic and Health Surveys in the years listed.
Source: Sahn, Stifel, and Younger 1999.

We present Gini coefficients, a popular measure of inequality, to describe how income inequality evolved in our sample of countries (table 5).[7] All underlying "welfare" measures are based on real total household expenditures.[8] The surveys were designed to enable comparisons over time within a country, although because of different survey designs caution is warranted in making comparisons across countries. Nonetheless, the differences in the degree of income inequality in our sample of countries are striking. At one extreme, Zimbabwe has a highly unequal distribution (a Gini ratio of over 0.6), reflecting unequal land distribution, which is a result in part of its colonial history. Income distributions in Ghana and Uganda are far more egalitarian.[9]

The picture is one of very little change in *overall* income inequality in these countries, except in Zambia. Reforms and growth have clearly not led to a significant deterioration in inequality, as popular belief would hold (Forsyth 2000). Nevertheless, these aggregate measures of inequality can be misleading. They may in fact mask a great deal of distributional change, an issue we review further in chapter 3.

TRENDS IN POVERTY DURING THE 1990s

If growth episodes were not associated with significant changes in inequality, did they lead to poverty reduction? Table 6 reports poverty estimates for the countries covered by the Poverty Dynamics in Africa Initiative. As with the inequality measures, real household consumption per adult equivalent (or in some cases, per capita) is taken as the central economic welfare measure. Poverty lines in all cases (except Mauritania) are derived from a food consumption basket, which is estimated to yield a minimum caloric intake, with adjustments made for essential nonfood consumption. These poverty lines are typically much higher than the purchasing power parity (PPP) US$1/day poverty line. The average poverty incidence in 24 spells of poverty change in African countries analyzed by Ravallion (2001) was 31 percent (based on the US$1/day line). This compares with (unweighted) average headcounts of 58 percent in our sample of nine spells. The country-based poverty lines in our countries are, therefore, significantly higher than the PPP US$1/day benchmark. Because of

Table 5. Consumption Inequality in Eight African Countries during the 1990s
(Gini coefficient)

Country and survey years	Year 1	Year 2	Change
Ethiopia 1994–97[a]			
Rural	0.43	0.42	−0.01
Urban	0.44	0.48	0.04
Ghana 1992–98			
Rural	0.34	0.37	0.03
Urban	0.34	0.35	0.01
All	0.37	0.39	0.02
Madagascar 1993–99			
Rural	0.42	0.36	−0.06
Urban	0.41	0.38	−0.03
All	0.43	0.38	−0.05
Mauritania 1987–95			
Rural	0.43	0.37	−0.06
Urban	0.40	0.36	−0.04
All	0.43	0.39	−0.04
Nigeria 1992–96			
Rural	0.51	0.44	−0.07
Urban	0.51	0.51	0.00
All	0.51	0.47	−0.04
Uganda 1992–2000			
Rural	0.33	0.32	−0.01
Urban	0.39	0.40	0.01
All	0.36	0.38	0.02
Zambia 1991–98			
Rural	0.61	0.48	−0.13
Urban	0.47	0.43	−0.04
All	0.58	0.48	−0.10
Zimbabwe 1991–96			
Rural	0.58	0.57	−0.01
Urban	0.60	0.59	−0.01
All	0.68	0.64	−0.04

Note: Real expenditures per adult equivalent. For urban Ethiopia, Nigeria, and Madagascar, real per capita expenditures were used.
a. Purposively sampled villages and urban centers—not nationally representative.
Source: Country studies completed under the Poverty Dynamics in Africa Initiative (see bibliography).

differences in survey design and in the specifics of how the welfare measure and poverty lines are derived, the data in table 6 are not comparable across countries. The research, however, has been designed to ensure comparable estimates over time.

Table 6. Consumption Poverty in Eight African Countries during the 1990s (percent)

Country and survey years	Poverty headcount (P_0)			Severity index (P_2)		
	Year 1	Year 2	Percentage change	Year 1	Year 2	Percentage change
Ethiopia[a]						
1989–95 (rural)	61	51	−16	17	12	−29
1994–97 (rural)	39	29	−26	8	6	−25
1994–97 (urban)	39	36	−8	—	—	—
Ghana						
1992–98	51	39	−24	9	7	−22
Madagascar						
1993–97	70	73	5	17	19	12
1997–99	73	71	−3	19	19	0
Mauritania						
1987–95	58	35	−40	17	6	−65
Nigeria						
1985–92	46	43	−7	8	9	13
1992–96	43	66	53	9	17	89
Uganda						
1992–97	56	44	−21	10	6	−40
1997–2000	44	35	−20	6	5	−16
Zambia						
1991–96	69	80	14	30	31	1
1996–98	80	76	−5	31	26	−16
Zimbabwe						
1991–96	26	35	35	4	5	25

— Not available.
a. The two rural samples are different and not comparable. They are based, respectively, on 6 and 15 purposively sampled rural villages for 1989–95 and 1994–97; urban figures are based on per capita household expenditures in seven large towns, including Addis Ababa and Dire Dawa, and are not nationally representative.
Source: World Bank data and country studies completed under the Poverty Dynamics in Africa Initiative (see bibliography).

The poverty measures we report here are derived from the familiar class of poverty indexes after Foster, Greer, and Thorbecke (1984). The general formula for these poverty measures is as follows:

$$(1) \qquad P_{\alpha} = \frac{1}{n} \sum_{i=1}^{q} \left(\frac{z - y_i}{z} \right)^{\alpha} \qquad \alpha \geq 0$$

where n is the total population, q the number of poor people, y_i the income (consumption) of individual i, z the poverty line, and α a "poverty aversion" parameter. The larger α is, the greater the weight placed on the very poorest people. If $\alpha = 0$, equation (1) becomes simply q/n, which is the *headcount ratio*, or the incidence of poverty. Estimates of the *headcount* (P_0) are reported in the first data panel of table 6. Setting $\alpha = 2$ involves taking the square of the proportionate poverty gap. This measure (P_2) is given in the second panel in table 6 and is sometimes known as the *severity index*. We report this index because it is sensitive to the distribution of income *among* the poor. It is particularly sensitive to changes in the living standards of the poorest of the poor. The data suggest the following:

- Most countries can be considered as having to deal with "mass" poverty. More than 70 percent of the people in Madagascar and Zambia were estimated to be poor, and 66 percent of Nigerians were estimated to be poor in 1996.
- There is no uniform trend. Although the incidence of consumption poverty declined substantially in several countries (Ethiopia, Ghana, Mauritania, and Uganda), it rose sharply in Nigeria and Zimbabwe. Poverty has fluctuated in Zambia and Madagascar, increasing marginally in the former and remaining more or less unchanged in the latter.
- Where the incidence of poverty has declined, the data suggest that the poorest sections of the population have also benefited. This is suggested by the significant downward trend in the severity index (P_2). In several cases the percentage fall in the P_2 measure was greater than that in P_0.

POVERTY, INEQUALITY, AND ECONOMIC GROWTH

In some cases these changes in poverty occurred in a context of economic decline (Nigeria and Zimbabwe, and Madagascar and Zambia during the earlier periods). In others they accompanied overall economic progress (Ethiopia, Ghana, Mauritania, and Uganda). To shed more light on the relationship between poverty, inequality, and growth, table 7 presents a decomposition of poverty incidence into two components: changes explained by changes in mean consumption (keeping the *distribution* of consumption unchanged), and those arising from changing consumption distribution (with the mean kept constant). The poverty measure that is decomposed in the table is the elasticity of headcount poverty with respect to changes in mean household expenditure.[10]

Table 7. Relative Importance of Mean and Distribution in the Evolution of Poverty Incidence

Country and survey years	Change in mean per capita expenditure (percent)	Change in poverty headcount (percent)	Poverty elasticity with respect to mean expenditure	Explained by changes in: [a]	
				Mean	Distribution
Ghana					
1992–98	23.7	−23.5	−0.99	−0.93	−0.06
Madagascar					
1993–97	−17.5	4.7	−0.27	−0.77	0.50
1997–99	0.6	−2.7	−4.51	−0.79	−3.72
Mauritania					
1987–95	49.5	−39.7	−0.81	−0.74	−0.07
Nigeria					
1992–96	−41.1	53.6	−1.30	−1.33	0.02
Uganda					
1992–97	17.1	−20.7	−1.21	−1.07	−0.15
Zambia					
1991–96	−25.7	14.5	−0.56	−0.56	0.00
1996–98	13.2	−4.6	−0.35	−0.43	0.08
Zimbabwe					
1991–96	−28.8	35.3	−1.23	−2.22	0.99

a. Decompositions are based on Kakwani and Pernia 2000.
Source: World Bank data and country studies completed under the Poverty Dynamics in Africa Initiative (see bibliography).

Overall, changes in poverty incidence are predominantly caused by changes in mean expenditure (table 7). Where there has been economic growth, both mean and redistribution effects typically have the same sign and have combined to reduce poverty (in Ghana, Mauritania, and Uganda). The mean effect largely dominates the redistribution effect, however. In contrast, where there has been recession, mean and redistribution effects typically have opposite signs, and the redistribution effect substantially mitigates the poverty-increasing impact of lower mean incomes (Madagascar, Nigeria, and Zimbabwe). Better-off groups clearly bear a heavier burden of income losses during periods of economic decline in Africa.[11]

To assess further the extent to which these episodes of growth and recession are pro-poor, we follow Kakwani and Pernia (2000) in defining

$$\phi = \frac{\eta}{\eta_g}$$

where η is the *observed* elasticity of headcount poverty with respect to changes in mean expenditure, and η_g is the elasticity of headcount poverty, assuming that the distribution of income did not change during the period. ϕ can be defined as an index of pro-poor growth. Growth can be considered pro-poor if $\phi > 1$.[12] Table 8 compares estimates of ϕ for these seven African countries with recent experience in Asia. On the basis of this sample of countries, growth and recession episodes in Africa have tended to be pro-poor, and indeed more so than the Asian experience.

Taking all nine spells of poverty change in our sample of African countries, we obtain a growth elasticity of poverty incidence of just –0.93 (figure 1).[13] Although growth is pro-poor, its quantitative impact on the headcount is limited in this sample because of the depth of poverty— large numbers are subsisting well below the poverty line (and poverty lines are set well above modal consumption). The growth elasticity of the severity index (P_2), at –1.42 (with a standard error of 0.35), is higher, which indicates that growth has improved the economic well-being of the poorest, although not enough to take them out of poverty.

As discussed above, countries with lower initial inequality typically grow more rapidly in subsequent years and experience greater poverty

Table 8. Pro-poor Growth Indexes (ϕ) for Selected African and Asian Countries in Selected Years

African country/survey years	ϕ	Asian country/survey years	ϕ
		Growth episodes	
Ghana 1992–98	1.07	Thailand 1992–96	0.61
Mauritania 1987–95	1.10	Lao PDR 1993–98	0.21
Uganda 1992–97	1.14	Korea 1990–96	1.03
Zambia 1996–98	0.82		
		Recession or stagnation episodes	
Madagascar 1993–97	2.85	Thailand 1996–98	0.73
Nigeria 1992–96	1.02	Korea 1997–98	0.84
Zambia 1991–96	1.00		
Zimbabwe 1991–96	1.81		

Note: For details of method, see text.   Asian country estimates are simple means across years within the subperiods shown. Lao PDR = Lao People's Democratic Republic.
Source: Table 7, Kakwani and Pernia 2000.

Figure 1. Relationship between Changes in Poverty and Mean Expenditure

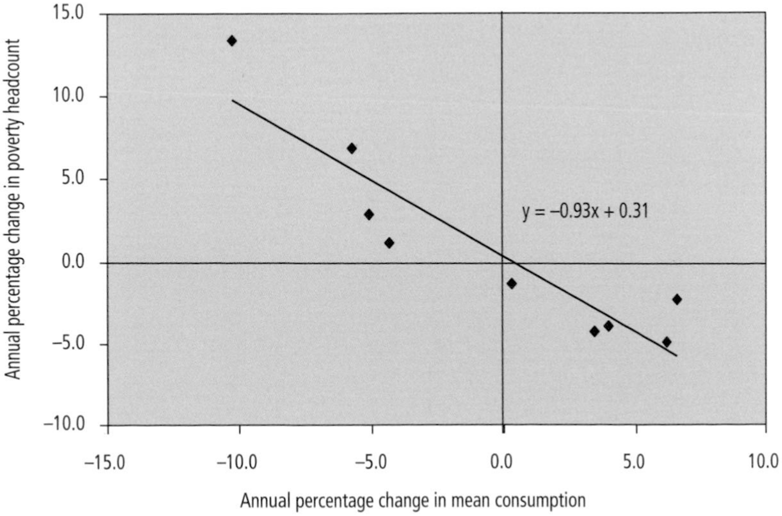

Source: Authors' calculations.

impact from that growth. The experience of this (albeit small) sample of African countries is consistent with this view (figure 2). The countries that had lower levels of initial inequality, as evidenced by the Gini ratios, were more likely to experience declines in poverty in subsequent years. That said, it is worth noting that the three countries with identical initial year Gini ratios (of 0.43)—Ethiopia, Mauritania, and Madagascar—experienced subsequent annual poverty changes of, respectively, –8.7, –5.0, and +0.2 percent. Although the pattern across countries suggests that higher levels of inequality are associated with lower subsequent growth and poverty reduction, there is sufficient variation around this empirical regularity to counsel caution.

Figure 2. Initial Inequality and Subsequent Poverty Trends

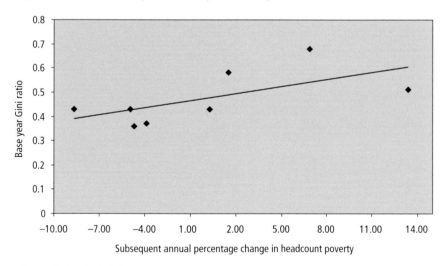

Source: Authors' calculations.

Growth and Systematic Changes in Income Distribution: A Macro Perspective

Our review of the evidence so far suggests that growth has been pro-poor in the African countries discussed in chapter 1. The changes have occurred during an era of economic policy reform, institutional change, and profound internal and external shocks, such as droughts, disease, and fluctuating commodity prices. These events have effects at all levels—they influence the growth rate of the economy at large, they affect the functioning of markets and of government, they change village and community life, and they impinge directly on the lives of households and individuals. Understanding how these changes have influenced poverty outcomes, therefore, calls for knowledge at both the macroeconomic (economywide) and microeconomic (household–individual) levels. This is the approach we take here. We first assess how macro-level changes (in economic and institutional environments) have affected poverty outcomes. This provides the context in which we then review (in chapter 3) the microeconomic evidence linking poverty outcomes to policies and shocks.

MACROECONOMIC REFORMS AND POVERTY TRENDS

We begin by reviewing the relationship between macroeconomic policy reforms and income poverty. To do so, we elaborate and update the analysis of Demery and Squire (1996) who examined the empirical association between improvements in macroeconomic balances and poverty reduction based on data of the late 1980s and the early 1990s. With better comparable household data now available (including emerging panel data) and with another decade of economic reform in many countries, we are in a good position to revisit this issue.[14]

Following Bouton, Jones, and Kiguel (1994) we calculate a macroeconomic policy index or score, based on changes in three key elements of sound macroeconomic policy: fiscal, monetary, and exchange rate policy. The overall macroeconomic policy score is a weighted average of these components, the weights being derived from international cross-sectional growth regressions. These scores are computed for the three-year period prior to each survey, and changes in the index are then compared. The index is so computed that increases in the score (either lower negative values or higher positive values) indicate an *improvement* in economic policy (table 9). Details of the changes in the different policy instrument indicators and the computations made in deriving the macroeconomic policy score are given in appendix table A3.

Given weaknesses in the underlying survey data, we prefer not to retain two countries included in the original Demery and Squire (1996) piece (Tanzania and Kenya). For Ethiopia, Ghana, and Nigeria, we update the estimates by introducing trends in the 1990s. Finally, we add the cases of Madagascar, Mauritania, Uganda, Zambia, and Zimbabwe to give an overall coverage of 15 episodes of change in nine countries. Most countries experienced improvements in their macroeconomic policy indicators—those for the second period (that is, the three-year period prior to the second survey) being generally better than those of the earlier period (the three years prior to the first survey). But there were only marginal improvements in Ghana (1992–98) and Zimbabwe (1991–96), however, and no change in Zambia (1996–98). Macroeconomic destabilization is observed in two countries—Côte d'Ivoire during the 1980s and Nigeria in the 1990s.

Table 9. Changes in Macroeconomic Policy Scores, Selected Countries

Country and computation period	Change during:			Average score	
	Fiscal policy	Monetary policy	Exchange rate policy	Unweighted	Weighted
Côte d'Ivoire					
1985–88	−3	1	−1	−1.0	−1.5
Ethiopia					
1989–95	−1	0.5	2.5	0.7	1.0
1994–97	2	1.5	2.5	2.0	2.2
Ghana					
1988–92	−1	1.5	2	0.8	0.8
1992–98	0	−0.5	0.5	0.0	0.2
Madagascar					
1993–97	0.0	−0.5	0.0	−0.2	−0.1
1997–99	1.0	1.0	0.0	0.7	0.5
Mauritania					
1987–95	3	0.5	2.5	2.0	2.4
Nigeria					
1985–92	1	−0.5	3	1.2	1.9
1992–96	1	−1	−2.5	−0.8	−1.0
Uganda					
1992–97	2	1.5	−0.5	1.0	0.7
1997–2000	0	0.5	0.5	0.3	0.3
Zambia					
1991–96	1	2	2	1.7	1.6
1996–98	1	1	−1	0.3	0.0
Zimbabwe					
1991–96	−1	−0.5	1.5	0.0	0.3

Sources: Demery and Squire 1996; authors' computations from World Bank data (see appendix table A3).

Setting these against the trends in poverty reduction (figure 3) confirms that countries achieving improvements in their macroeconomic balances in Africa typically have not experienced (in the aggregate at least) increases in consumption poverty—rather the reverse.[15] Of the 15 episodes of change for which we have data, 9 episodes indicate both macroeconomic policy improvement and subsequent poverty reduction. In the two cases where macroeconomic balances substantially deteriorated, poverty is indicated to have increased sharply. Only 2 of the 15 observations (Zimbabwe, 1991–96, and Zambia, 1991–96) are in the "wrong" quadrant in figure 3 (improved macroeconomic policy and increased poverty).

The *association* between the macroeconomic policy stance and poverty reduction does not necessarily imply any cause or direct behavioral link.[16] Rather, this evidence serves to highlight the close interactions between macroeconomic policies and economic well-being at the household level. An important feature missing from this analysis is any measure of policy persistence and consistency.[17] Collier and Gunning (1999) argue that the slow investment response to the reforms in part derives from a fear of policy reversals. Countries with a longer history of consistent policies (Ethiopia, Ghana, Mauritania, and Uganda in our sample) are more likely to experience growth and poverty reduction dividends from the reforms.[18] And the macroeconomic analysis is partial in another respect—the changes in the macroeconomic accounts took place alongside other reforms—mostly of a "structural" nature (trade liberalization, agricultural marketing reforms, privatization, and so on)—and changing

Figure 3. Macroeconomic Policy Reform and Poverty Trends

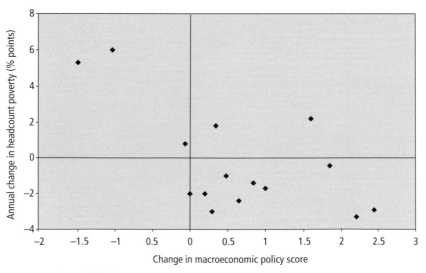

Source: Authors' calculations.

institutional environments. Both the institutional environment and the sectoral reforms are certain to be important as well, as is illustrated by the occurrence of similar poverty reductions among some of the countries, despite quite different changes in their macroeconomic indicators (see southeast quadrant in figure 3).

INSTITUTIONAL CHANGE AND POVERTY TRENDS

There is an accumulation of convincing empirical evidence pointing to the importance of political stability and good governance for growth and poverty reduction (Alesina and Perotti 1994; Collier 1999; Collier and Gunning 1999; Knack and Keefer 1995; World Bank 2000). Although the construction and consolidation of good indicators of political stability and good governance remain works in progress, the composite political risk index of the International Country Risk Guide (ICRG), and subsets thereof, have been frequently used by researchers to examine the effect of governance and institutional quality on growth and poverty. The composite index consists of 12 components covering different aspects of political stability (for example, government stability, internal conflict, and external conflict), governance, and institutional quality (for example, corruption, democratic accountability, and bureaucracy quality). The key advantage of the ICRG index is its broad coverage across countries and over time (1985 to current).[19] Evaluations of the different aspects of the index are provided by a private consultancy.

We find an improvement in the political risk score during all episodes of poverty change covered by the Poverty Dynamics in Africa Initiative.[20] In Ethiopia (1989–95) the improvement followed largely from reduced risk of internal and external conflict following peace agreements with Eritrea. Better overall governance (as captured by the corruption, law and order, democratic accountability, and bureaucratic quality indexes), as well as greater government stability and reduced risk of internal conflicts, drove progress in institutional quality in Ghana (1992–98) and Uganda (1992–97). Increased government stability was responsible for the change in Madagascar. And in Zimbabwe (1991–96) the improvement followed from reduced risk of an external conflict, a result of the end of the Cold War and the peace process in neighboring Mozambique. Greater external security is also an important factor in explaining the large improvement in the political risk score in Zambia, in addition to the substantial progress in internal political stability and security (law and order) following the peaceful handover of power by Kenneth Kaunda in 1991 after 27 years of autocratic rule.

Plotting the changes in the average annual political risk scores of the survey years of our countries against annual changes in the observed poverty incidence (figure 4) suggests that improvements in political stability and governance are generally associated with reductions in poverty, although experiences vary across countries.[21] In 9 out of the 13 episodes these improvements were accompanied by poverty reduction. In one episode we observe a modest increase in poverty (Madagascar during 1993–97), whereas in the three other cases (Nigeria, Zambia during 1991–96, and Zimbabwe) the poverty increase was more pronounced. In Nigeria the recorded improvement in the institutional environment was marginal (3.3 points) and was in all likelihood swamped by the adverse effects of the macroeconomic deterioration in the 1991–96 period. The other exceptions, Zambia and Zimbabwe, are more of a puzzle. The macroeconomic balances also improved during this 1991–96 episode of poverty increase (albeit only modestly in Zimbabwe). So where did things go wrong? The answer to this cannot be provided here, but the very high initial inequality in both Zambia and Zimbabwe was a particularly serious challenge for growth and poverty reduction during the decade. Also, both countries experienced severe droughts in 1994, followed by mediocre rainfall in 1995, which left households under considerable stress. This compares with above-average rainfall in 1990, the year preceding the first survey. We discuss the Zimbabwe episode of poverty increase and the role of rainfall shocks in further detail below.

Although our measures of political stability and the quality of governance are admittedly crude, these findings would support the general observation that increased political stability and improved governance go hand in hand with poverty reduction. Nevertheless, many difficult questions remain to be resolved. Which of the different components of institutional change (for example, political, economic, civil rights, or social stability) have had the most significant impact? And what is the direction of causality and the channels through which institutional improvements and poverty reduction may affect each other (Aron 2000)? These fall beyond the scope of this study.

Figure 4. Change in Political Stability and Governance and Poverty Trends

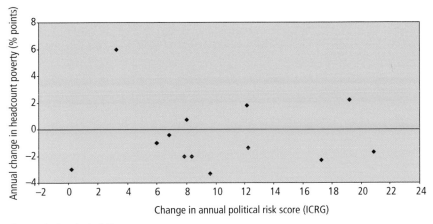

Source: Authors' calculations.

Growth and Systematic Changes in Income Distribution: A Micro Perspective

The evidence from the African experience covered in this study indicates that growth and recession have been pro-poor. Yet this conclusion must be qualified—it is true only in an aggregate sense. Further decomposition of national inequality and poverty measures—by geographical location and socioeconomic group—indicates that the aggregate statistics often mask a wide variety of experience. Some groups and regions gained disproportionately from the newly created opportunities following economic reforms, whereas others lost out or even became impoverished. Similarly, overall Gini coefficients often appear stable over time despite substantial churning within and across geographical regions, as illustrated by the experience in Ghana (discussed below). This suggests that the positive association between improved macroeconomic environments and poverty reduction is conditioned by other factors, such as location and infrastructure, households' private and public endowments, and the occurrence of shocks.

To disentangle the effects of these disparate events and factors on the different sections of African society, it is tempting to use economywide modeling techniques. They can generate counterfactuals and provide insights into the respective impacts of policies and other shocks. Much of the serious work to date on policy reform and poverty in Africa has relied on such modeling approaches (Bourguignon and Morrisson 1992; Sahn, Dorosh, and Younger 1997). Yet, despite their advantages, these approaches also have a number of important limitations. The models typically impose a strong structure, which sometimes leads to questions about their realism. They are most often calibrated at one point in time. As a result, they cannot always confidently track changes over time—the economic history. Indeed, such history usually involves policy-induced structural changes in the economy that are not captured in such experiments.

By exploiting different experiences across households, this chapter places emphasis instead on the microeconometric evidence emerging from the much improved and richer household survey data sets. We begin by highlighting two Poverty Dynamics panel studies—Dercon (2002) on Ethiopia, and Deininger and Okidi (2001) on Uganda. Focusing on the factors they highlight as key for economic growth and poverty reduction, we then assess the evidence from the other case studies that use either repeated cross-sectional regressions (Ghana, Madagascar, Zimbabwe) or simply an extensively documented narrative linking the macroeconomic events to the observed evolutions in household welfare (Mauritania and Zambia).

The Ethiopia and Uganda studies are particularly informative for two reasons. First, both involve the use of panel data, which track changes in the living standards of the same households over much of the 1990s. Although not identical, both the methodologies they adopt and their results are similar. Second, both countries experienced far-reaching reforms in economic policy, inducing changes in market institutions, relative prices, and producer behavior. The rural sector in Ethiopia had previously been largely ignored and heavily taxed. Yet in the early 1990s agricultural reforms were initiated, including the abolition of food delivery quotas for farmers and a relaxation (and later abolition) of restrictions on private grain trades. These measures substantially reduced the food marketing margins between surplus and deficit regions. The birr was devalued by 142 percent and the foreign exchange markets were liberalized. This positively affected the farmgate prices of tradables, such as coffee and *chat* (a popular, mild narcotic), although the effect was somewhat muted because of the existence of parallel markets. Producer prices for coffee evolved favorably during the period, partly because of an increase in the world price.

Uganda's rural sector lost considerable ground during the period up to 1985. Adversely affected by state intervention, civil strife, and agricultural price disincentives (through overvalued exchange rates and the implicit taxation of state marketing boards), rural producers retreated into subsistence. The production of cotton, tea, and coffee suffered accordingly. From the late 1980s on, government policy changed, dismantling the biases against rural producers. Coffee marketing and exports were liberalized, and direct export taxation was abandoned. Similar measures were taken in the cotton sector. The foreign exchange market was liberalized, leading to real exchange rate depreciation. The weighted real producer price of export crops in Uganda (77 percent of which are coffee) increased by 78 percent between 1989–91 and 1995–97. Decomposition of this increase indicates that changes in the nominal protection coefficient (producer price or border price), changes in the real exchange rate, and changes in the real world price contributed, respectively, 58, 9, and 11 percent (Townsend 1999). During the past decade, agricultural output has recovered, averaging between 4 and 4.5 percent per year in real terms. This growth has played an important role in reducing poverty (Appleton and others 1999).

In sum, economic policy reforms in both Ethiopia and Uganda had significant effects on agricultural markets and the prices farmers received for both food and export crops. At the same time, however, the period witnessed other changes, including rainfall variation. Both Dercon (2002) and Deininger and Okidi (2001) use the panel data to assess how these different changes affected household incomes and consumption, and rural poverty.

Dercon (2002) uses panel data from six *rural* communities in Ethiopia covering the period 1989–95.[22] The change in household real consumption per adult is explained through a reduced form regression model with a Oaxaca-Blinder type decomposition. In this approach changes in consumption and poverty can be explained by changes in endowments over time and changes in returns to endowments. The main regressors were changes in real crop producer prices (which Dercon 2002 shows to be closely related to the macroeconomic and agricultural reforms that were implemented during the period), location (proxied by distance to an urban center), access to roads, private endowments (land, labor, and education), and two shock variables, rainfall and ill health. His results are summarized in table 10.

Household consumption increased on average by 32 percent between 1989 and 1995, and poverty—here defined as poverty gap in logs—decreased by 29 percentage points. The growth in rural household incomes has been largely fueled by changes in relative crop prices and

Table 10. Decomposition of Consumption Growth per Adult and Poverty Gap Ratio, Ethiopia (percent)

Item	Actual		Counterfactual: No reform and peace		Counterfactual: No risk	
	Growth	Poverty	Growth	Poverty	Growth	Poverty
Real crop price change	15	−18	n.a.	n.a.	15	−16
Change in returns to road access/location	19	−23	n.a.	n.a.	19	−21
Private endowments						
Increase in land	7	−10	1	−2	7	−8
Change in returns to land	3	0	n.a.	n.a.	3	−1
Increases in adult labor	3	−4	3	−4	3	−4
Changes in returns to educated adults	0	0	n.a.	n.a.	0	0
Change in adult equivalent units	−5	7	−5	7	−5	7
Shocks						
Relative rainfall shock	−8	13	−8	14	n.a.	n.a.
Illness shocks	−4	5	−4	5	n.a.	n.a.
Residual	0	0	0	3	0	0
Percentage growth and percentage point poverty change (sum of above)	32	−29	−13	23	42	−44

n.a. Not applicable.
Source: Dercon 2002.

increased returns to location and access to road infrastructure.[23] This is clearly illustrated by Dercon's (2002) simulations, which show that consumption would have *declined* by 13 percent and poverty would have *increased* by 23 percent had there been no peace and no economic and agricultural reforms.[24] Interestingly, all poor households (even those that fell into poverty) benefited from the relative price changes that occurred. Those that escaped poverty benefited most, however. These findings suggest that the reforms and increased political stability substantially improved the well-being of the poor, both directly through a favorable change in relative prices and indirectly through an increase in the returns to market connectedness as determined by road infrastructure and distance to urban centers.

In addition to public endowments, such as road infrastructure and location, private endowments are also found to be important for consumption growth and poverty reduction. Increases in land holdings (through redistribution) or improvements in the quality of the land owned, and increases in adult labor reduced poverty by 14 percentage points.[25] Returns to land also increased, but because the poor typically possess little (and often less fertile) land, they profited much less than the average household from the increased returns to land.[26] Finally, the occurrence of shocks (especially rainfall, but also illness shocks) had a large negative effect both on the growth process and on poverty outcomes. If households had had access to full insurance protection from rainfall and health shocks, poverty would have declined by 42 percentage points compared with 29 percentage points in its absence. Dercon (2002) shows that the reason why households fell into poverty during this period was mainly the combined effects of the rainfall and illness shocks. Agricultural marketing reforms are shown to have benefited even the households that lost ground during the period.

In sum, households that escaped poverty during the period not only benefited from better producer prices, they also enjoyed a more favorable location and were endowed with good access to infrastructure and better land. Those that remained poor or that fell into poverty did so in part because they were badly placed in terms of location and land. They were also at the receiving end of particularly bad luck—they suffered most from poor rainfall and from ill health.

Deininger and Okidi (2001) analyze changes in consumption and income observed for a panel of about 1,200 Ugandan households during the period 1992–2000. They regress household-level changes in consumption and income against variables representing the change in relative producer prices of coffee, their access to infrastructure, their initial endowments of physical and human capital, the initial health status of households, and their social capital. They found these variables to be significant in explaining growth in Ugandan household incomes during the 1990s. As in Ethiopia, the effect of changes in relative prices—in this case an increase in farmgate coffee prices largely brought about by market liberalization, but also by the devaluation and favorable world prices—on consumption growth was substantial.

Initial private endowments of education and other assets (mainly land) were also crucial for consumption growth. For example, if households had had six years of completed schooling on average (instead of the observed three years)—equivalent to completing primary schooling—growth in consumption would have been 2 percentage points higher. A difference of one standard deviation in initial asset value (about half of which is accounted for by land) put households on a 2 percentage point higher consumption growth path. Households that in 1992 were afflicted by health problems—related to malaria in over 80 percent of cases—experienced consumption growth, which was, other things being constant, 1.8 percentage points lower than those not experiencing such problems. Households with access to electricity enjoyed consumption growth that was 6 percentage points higher than in other households.

The above results offer insight into what determined the growth in income and consumption among Ugandan households. How did such growth affect poverty? To address this, Deininger and Okidi (2001) estimate a multinomial logit model of changes in poverty status—households are classified as not changing their status, falling into poverty, or escaping from poverty. They find that the relative coffee price changes had a powerful poverty-reducing impact, indicating that their effect was broad-based and that price changes in tradable commodities directly benefited poor producers—and not only indirectly through the labor market. Moreover, households with higher education, more initial assets (such as land), better health, and better access to infrastructure (such as electricity) and location (distance to municipality) were far less likely than others to fall into poverty and more likely to escape from it.

The results from these microeconometric analyses of panel data point to the following factors that appear to influence the relationship between economic growth and poverty reduction:

- Many rural households stand to benefit directly from liberalization measures, as well as increased political stability and better governance—and the gains can be substantial. Insofar as liberalization measures increase producer prices, rural producers will gain, and to the extent that food marketing margins tend to decline, rural consumers will gain as well. Nonetheless, some will gain more than others, depending on the product and consumption mix of the household.

- A household's location is key in conditioning the extent to which it will benefit from liberalization measures. Specifically, whether the household had access to infrastructure and urban markets was an immensely important factor in governing the growth in household income. It explains about half of household consumption growth and poverty reduction in Ethiopia during 1989–95, and it was also quantitatively important for growth in Ugandan household income. So, connectedness to markets as captured by access to infrastructure (especially roads, but also electricity) and distance to urban centers is likely to be a major factor in determining how growth in any country transmits its benefits to the population.

- The potential for economic growth and poverty reduction further depends on a household's private endowments. Households with larger private endowments—be it more and better qualified labor or land—not only tend to be less poor, they are also better placed to profit from new opportunities generated by liberalization and institutional change.

- It is vital to separate out the effect of shocks when assessing the role of policy changes. Dercon (2002) highlights rainfall and health shocks, both of which are certain to be relevant to poor households in most African countries. The importance of health shocks is also underscored by Deininger and Okidi (2001) for the Ugandan case. Export commodity price fluctuations, although not explicitly treated in these studies, form another important risk factor.

We now examine the evidence on distribution and poverty changes in other countries covered in this review and look for echoes of the findings from the panel data of Ethiopia and Uganda.

LIBERALIZATION

The changes in relative prices through exchange rate devaluations, the opening of domestic markets, and changes in the structure of production are certain to lead to shifts in income distribution, with producers of tradable goods (mostly exportables) benefiting directly from the economic policy reforms. The studies of Uganda and Ethiopia show that these effects were evident during the 1990s and that they directly benefited poor households. The experience of Ghana in West Africa echoes these East African findings. Ghana experienced sharp poverty reductions among cash (export) crop producers during the 1990s, a result of more favorable world cocoa prices and an increase in cocoa production. Table 11 compares trends in poverty among crop producers in rural Ghana and Uganda.

In both countries about two-fifths of the population are food-producing farmers, of whom about two-thirds were poor in the early 1990s. In both countries, poverty fell among food producers, but the decline was not as great as that experienced by export crop producers. Most of the

Table 11. Poverty (P_0) Incidence by Rural Activity, Ghana and Uganda in the 1990s

	Ghana				Uganda			
Rural activity	Population share (1998)	P_0 1992	1998	Percent reduction	Population share (2000)	P_0 1992	2000	Percent reduction
Food crop	43.9	68.1	59.4	−12.8	45.9	63.3	45.7	−27.8
Cash crop	6.3	64.0	38.7	−39.5	21.3	62.7	29.7	−52.6

Source: Appleton 2001; Coulombe and McKay 2001.

rural poor appear to have benefited from growth, but those producing export crops have benefited the most. A much larger share of the population in Uganda grows cash crops (21 percent) than that in Ghana (6 percent), which may explain the larger drop in poverty among food crop producers in Uganda. Reviewing the existing evidence on the experience with agricultural reforms in Sub-Saharan Africa, Kherallah and others (2000) arrive at a similar conclusion—export crop producers seem to have benefited more than did food crop producers. What needs to be better understood is the *transmission* mechanism that led to economic gains of households not producing for export.

Potential pathways include rural labor markets, with higher export crop prices stimulating export crop production leading to increased demand for agricultural wage labor and ultimately higher agricultural real wages. Abdulai and Delgado (2000) find that in Ghana, a 1 percent change in the domestic terms of trade between agriculture and nonagriculture leads to a 0.83 percent change in the real agricultural wage rate in the long term, underscoring the importance of labor markets in transmitting the effects of economic reforms. Increased liquidity in rural economies from agricultural exports can also have important spin-off effects, through an expansion of both investment in export and food crop production and increased consumption of goods and services produced with previously underutilized local labor, land, or capital. As a rule of thumb Delgado and others (1998) posit that any policy enhancing producers' income from agricultural exports increases local rural income by twice the amount of the increased exports.

To understand the different evolution in poverty among food and cash crop producers, it is important to keep in mind that the former group tends to be much more heterogeneous than the latter. In export crop–growing regions, the effects of favorable export crop prices were transmitted to the food-crop growing households—either through the labor market or the input and product markets, or both. Transmission of such benefits to areas unsuitable for export crop production, especially when they are also remote, is much harder. For example, in Ghana food producers in more remote and less integrated regions (in the north) did not experience a similar reduction in their poverty as did food growers in cash crop (and better integrated) areas. Similarly, food crop producers in

northern Uganda, which is also less accessible, appear not to have benefited from recent growth.

Periods of economic stagnation and recession also systematically
affect some groups more than others. In Zimbabwe, for example, the
increase in rural poverty during 1990–91 and 1995–96 was felt most
keenly among the commercial farmers (table 12). Disentangling exactly
why some suffered more than others is a difficult undertaking. Some
farmers might have suffered more than others from the drought (an issue
taken up by Alwang, Mills, and Taruvinga 2002 and discussed below). It
is also likely that the fall in incomes among commercial farmers was
caused by the decline in real tobacco prices, estimated by Townsend
(1999) to be –2.5 percent per year during 1990 and 1996–97. Other features of real price changes during the period identified by Townsend
(notably the increase in the real price of cotton and continued government intervention in the maize market) may also explain why the small-
holder group of farmers has not suffered as much as the commercial
farmers during this episode of drought and economic decline.

Table 12. Incidence of Rural Poverty by Farming Category, Zimbabwe, 1990–96

	Expenditure/adult equivalent					
	1990–91		1995–96		Percentage change in:	
Farming category	Mean consumption (Z$ 1990/ month)	Poverty headcount (percent)	Mean consumption (Z$ 1990/ month)	Poverty headcount (percent)	Mean consumption	Poverty headcount
Communal	65.54	38.5	50.17	52.0	–0.23	35.1
Small-scale commercial	93.15	18.7	65.95	34.4	–0.29	84.0
Large-scale commercial	99.21	16.3	76.85	27.4	–0.23	68.1
Resettlement areas	57.51	47.0	46.47	50.6	–0.19	7.7
Rural	69.60	35.8	54.29	48.0	–0.22	34.1

Source: Alwang and Ersado 1999.

LOCATION

The panel analysis of Ethiopian and Ugandan households provides strong empirical evidence that location is important in determining how growth influences income distribution. Other countries also experienced strongly divergent patterns in inequality across regions. In Ghana, for example, inequality fell sharply in Accra and in urban savannah and rural forest areas, whereas it increased sharply in the coastal zone and rural savannah. Our conclusion is that overall indexes of inequality can mask important changes in distribution—particularly across and within geographic regions.

Geography is even more important in explaining poverty trends. In some countries the decline in poverty is observed in both rural and urban areas (Ghana, Mauritania, and Uganda—table 13). In others, the change is confined mainly to urban areas (Zambia between 1991 and 1996). It is clear from the case studies that within both the rural and the urban sectors, poverty changes have varied considerably depending on geographical location. Some geographical areas have not benefited as much as others from growth, and some have even lost ground during the period of recovery. The different experience in the evolution of poverty seems closely related to the extent to which the region or village is integrated within the overall economy. The experiences of Ghana and Madagascar are illustrative.

Poverty in Accra fell sharply, but not in other urban areas (figure 5). In the savannah zone, poverty increased in both urban and rural areas, especially in the northern region and among subsistence farmers.[28] The fact that growth in Ghana saw aggregate poverty fall is very little comfort to food farmers and urban workers in the north of the country, who probably compare their fortunes with Accra residents. Important clues as to why Ghanaians in the north did not benefit from growth are found in recent papers by Badiane and Shively (1998) and Abdulai (2000), which conclude that markets (more specifically the maize market) in the more remote northern region are not very well integrated with the economy at large. This lack of integration most likely impeded the transmission of the benefits of growth to the region.

"Remoteness" is also important in understanding geographical differences in poverty outcomes in Madagascar. Paternostro, Razafindravonona,

Table 13. Headcount Poverty Trends in Rural and Urban Areas of Seven African Countries during the 1990s

Country and survey years	Population share in year 1 (%)	Rural			Urban		
		Year 1 (%)	Year 2 (%)	Change (% points)	Year 1 (%)	Year 2 (%)	Change (% points)
Ghana							
1992–98	67	64	49	−15	28	19	−9
Madagascar							
1993–99	81	75	77	2	50	52	2
Mauritania							
1987–95	56	68	48	−20	45	17	−28
Nigeria							
1992–96	62	46	69	23	37	58	21
Uganda							
1992–97	88	59	48	−11	28	16	−12
Zambia							
1991–96	62	88	90	2	47	62	15
1996–98	62	90	86	−4	62	59	−3
Zimbabwe							
1991–96	63	36	48	12	3	8	5

Source: World Bank, country studies completed under the Poverty Dynamics in Africa Initiative (see bibliography).

and Stifel (2001) disaggregate poverty according to an index of remoteness, the latter being a weighted sum of indicators reflecting access to roads, bus stops, agricultural extension services, modern fertilizers, and distance to schools and health facilities (the weights were derived from factor analysis). Their findings (table 14) indicate an association between the degree of remoteness and the likelihood of being in poverty. They also show that although rural poverty indicators were largely unchanged during 1997 and 1999, households assessed to be the most remote experienced increased poverty—in contrast with the least remote quintile, where poverty indicators actually improved.

Figure 5. Incidence of Consumption Poverty by Zone, Ghana, 1992–98

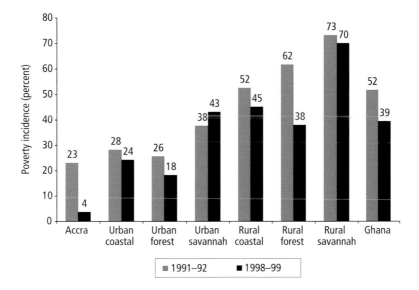

Source: Coulombe and McKay 2001.

Table 14. Rural Poverty by "Degree of Remoteness," Madagascar

Measure	Headcount (P_0)		Depth (P_1)	
	1997	1999	1997	1999
Total rural	76.0	76.7	34.7	36.1
Quintile of "remoteness index"				
Most remote	78.0	82.8	34.8	42.4
Second quintile	78.2	78.9	38.1	35.6
Third quintile	74.5	78.9	32.7	37.7
Fourth quintile	77.0	77.7	36.6	36.5
Least remote	72.6	65.9	31.6	29.0

Source: Paternostro, Razafindravonona, and Stifel 2001.

PRIVATE ENDOWMENTS

The experiences in Ethiopia and Uganda demonstrated that better-endowed households, particularly more educated households and those with more fertile land, were not only less likely to be poor, but also more likely to benefit from favorable changes in the macroeconomic environment. The importance of education for poverty reduction is echoed by the microeconometric evidence from Ghana, Madagascar, and Zimbabwe.[28] Both in Ghana and in Madagascar, real consumption levels increase with educational attainment. The returns to education across the different education levels increased from the first to the second survey year. These observations hold for both urban and rural areas. In Zimbabwe, a more precipitous increase in poverty following the economic decline was prevented because of previous investments in schooling that increased the educational attainment of the population in the 1990s (Alwang, Mills, and Taruvinga 2002). That incomes fell and poverty increased despite household efforts to invest in human capital, assets and migration can only be attributed to a reduction in the *rates of return* to these assets.

Evidence from Madagascar, the only other study that explicitly addresses the role of land holdings, confirms that consumption levels are higher for those who possess land, except for those with only a very small amount of land (less than 0.1 hectare per capita). Returns to land holdings also increase with the size of the plots owned. Returns to land holdings deteriorated from 1993 to 1999 for households with less than 0.4 hectare per capita, whereas they improved for those with more land. The changes in returns decreased poverty incidence among the latter group by 2 percentage points, whereas it increased poverty among the former by 0.82 percentage point. Paternostro, Razafindravonona, and Stifel (2001) surmise that this difference follows from more extensive land use by smallholders in the face of demographic pressures forcing small farmers to expand their fields into less productive and more fragile areas.

SHOCKS

Poverty estimates provide a snapshot of the standard of living at a certain point in time and reflect both policy reforms and temporary external shocks, such as droughts. When evaluating the evolution of poverty, it is thus important to control for the effect of external shocks on comparative poverty figures. Controlling for all other factors, the Ethiopian panel analysis estimated that household income growth was reduced by about a fifth because of rainfall shortage (Dercon 2002). The role of rainfall variations in influencing household income growth was also an important feature of the Zimbabwean and Madagascar experience.

That poverty increased sharply in Zimbabwe during the 1990s is without question (Alwang, Mills, and Taruvinga 2002). The decline in economic well-being and increase in poverty are evident from the leftward shift in the distribution of real household consumption (figure 6). The change occurred mainly in the vicinity of the poverty line (Z$30 per month)—with a sharp increase in the numbers of people consuming just below the poverty line and a parallel decline in the numbers just above it. What is less clear is whether poverty increased because of the droughts that afflicted the country in 1991–92 and again in 1994–95, or because of the Economic Structural Adjustment Program (launched in 1991) that was being implemented at the same time. Alwang, Mills, and Taruvinga (2002) apply nonparametric methods to simulate what the 1995 distribution would have been if the 1990 rainfall patterns had applied that year. This exercise confirms that the drought led to an increase in poverty during the early 1990s, but it also indicates that the drought alone cannot fully explain the deterioration in economic well-being (figure 7, panel A). As discussed before, actual changes in household location, assets, and individual characteristics (notably the levels of educational attainment) would actually, other things constant, have *raised* consumption levels and reduced poverty (figure 7, panel B). Without such changes, incomes would have deteriorated even more than they did.

Evidence from Madagascar further underscores the importance of weather shocks in comparing poverty over time. Simulations indicate that 75 percent of the predicted change in household economic well-being and poverty incidence can be traced back to the relative change in drought occurrence between 1993 and 1999. The insurance capacity of households against covariate shocks in many parts of Africa is extremely limited.

Figure 6. Shift in Welfare Distribution, Zimbabwe, 1990–95

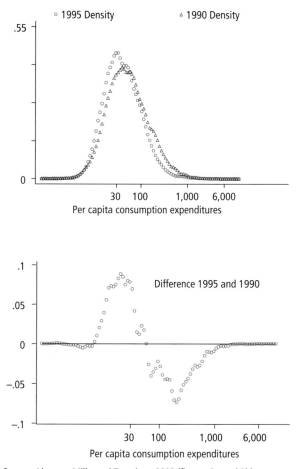

Source: Alwang, Mills, and Taruvinga 2002 (figures 3a and 3b).

Figure 7. Simulated Effects of Rainfall and Household Characteristics on Changes in the Welfare Distribution, Zimbabwe, 1990–95

A. Effects of rainfall (rural distribution only)

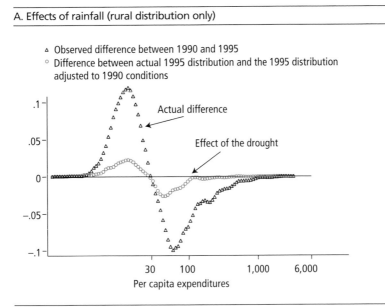

B. Effects of individual and household characteristics

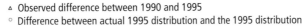

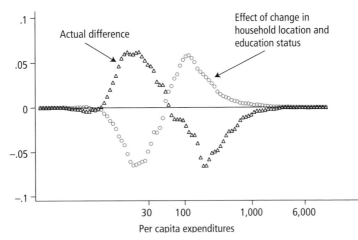

Source: Alwang, Mills, and Taruvinga 2002 (figures 10b and 9b, respectively).

CHAPTER 4

Concluding Remarks

The evidence of the 1990s provides ground for cautious optimism. In the aggregate at least, episodes of growth have contributed to reducing poverty in Africa, and countries that have experienced a recovery in their macroeconomic balances and the quality of their institutions have seen the numbers in poverty decline. There are three serious qualifications, however. First, experiences have varied enormously. Some countries have enjoyed a decade of sustained growth, and others have had to cope with crisis and decline. In the eight countries covered by the Poverty Dynamics in Africa Initiative, four experienced significant declines in poverty (Ethiopia, Ghana, Mauritania, and Uganda), two faced sharp increases (Nigeria and Zimbabwe), and in two (Madagascar and Zambia) there was no discernible trend, the outcome depending on the specific circumstances (rainfall, terms of trade) of the survey years in question.

The second qualification derives from the need to go beyond the averages. Although it is true that *overall* income distributions (evidenced by the Gini ratio) have not changed during African episodes of growth, and that such growth (or recession) can be characterized as pro-poor in this aggregate sense, this can be misleading. Beneath the aggregate numbers exists a variety of experiences. Neglect of this reality by policymakers— and sometimes also academics—has often impeded a constructive and fruitful dialogue with "civil society" about appropriate poverty-reducing policies (Kanbur 2001). Third, the Poverty Dynamics work highlights the importance of taking different perspectives of poverty. Although trends in human development indicators are generally consistent with economic well-being, their dynamics have been quite different in some countries. The multifaceted nature of poverty calls for multivariate approaches to tracking and understanding its dynamics.

Focusing on income poverty, our review of the evidence shows that there have been systematic changes in income distributions and poverty in the countries covered. We have identified some of the main contours of these distribution changes and highlighted four key policy messages: the importance of economic reform and political stability for poverty reduction; the role of location and remoteness in conditioning how the benefits of growth are distributed; the significance of private endowments (especially education and land) for the ability of households to take advantage of new opportunities, and the consequent poverty outcomes; and finally the need to account for shocks in understanding distributional outcomes and poverty changes over time.

The "emerging picture" described by Demery and Squire (1996) appears to be confirmed with the better data (reflecting also a longer time perspective than previous work). Improvements in the macroeconomic balances are associated with reductions in poverty in the region. There is also an emerging microeconomic picture concerning the consumption poverty impact of market liberalization. The analyses of household panel data by Dercon (2002) for Ethiopia and Deininger and Okidi (2001) for Uganda provide the most systematic and empirically convincing cases that policy-induced changes in relative prices can have poverty-reducing effects. Microeconomic evidence from Ghana provides some corroboration from West Africa.

The second policy message is the need for a geographical perspective on poverty. Although the various rounds of poverty assessments have established that the incidence of poverty varies considerably across different regions of a country, this recent work on poverty dynamics has shown that some regions, by virtue of their sheer remoteness, have been left behind somewhat as growth has picked up. Households with limited access to markets and public services have not benefited from growth during the 1990s. Public policy and the provision of public goods (notably infrastructure services—from the Ethiopian case, especially roads, and from the Ugandan case, electricity) must address these fundamental regional inequalities.

Third, both education and access to land emerge as key private endowments to enable households to escape poverty. The importance of education for poverty reduction is brought out in all our case studies—in rural and urban areas—with the marginal returns to education typically increasing by educational attainment. Although land redistributions may not be appropriate in all countries, as argued by Dercon (2002) for Ethiopia, it is ultimately the productive capacity of land that matters. A more efficient organization of agricultural services and agricultural inputs, such as fertilizer, could go a long way toward improving the productivity of land (Kherallah and others 2000).

Finally, the empirical evidence reviewed here underscores the importance of social protection in a poverty reduction strategy. Ill health and the impact of rainfall variations are the two risk factors featured. Dercon (2002) estimates that poverty reduction in the sample of Ethiopian rural communities would have been 18 percentage points greater had households been protected from the effects of ill health and rainfall shortages. The importance of weather shocks for poverty changes was also underscored by the findings from Zimbabwe and Madagascar. Deininger and Okidi (2001) find that ill health among Ugandans back in 1992 noticeably increased the probability of being in poverty eight years later. And in light of households' greater exposure to the vagaries of world commodity prices following liberalization, policies to help the poor manage their risks have become even more important nowadays.

Background Information on Data Sources

The core objective of the Poverty Dynamics studies was to investigate poverty changes over time, using the much improved household survey data base in Africa. For this, comparable measures of household economic "welfare" or well-being are called for. Issues of data comparability and the construction of a reliable welfare measure, therefore, have been central in each of the Poverty Dynamics studies. In this appendix we present some basic information on the survey instruments and the construction of the welfare measures used in the studies covered by the book. Although readers are referred to the individual studies for a detailed exposition of survey design and methodological choices made in building each individual welfare measure, we report here on some of their salient features.

SURVEYS USED

For all countries investigated, data were obtained from household surveys collected by local statistical authorities—the only exception being

Ethiopia where the authors constructed a purposively selected panel germane to their research objectives (in a collaborative venture with the University of Addis Ababa). Table A1 reports details on the survey design, time frame, coverage, and sample size. With the exception of Ethiopia, where the two panels used in the study covered only 6 and 15 villages, respectively, all the surveys are nationally representative. A few omissions, however, are worth noting in interpreting the results presented. The surveys used in Mauritania did not sample the nomadic population (about 6 percent in 2000). In Uganda the 1996–97 Monitoring Survey and the 1999–2000 Uganda National Household Survey did not cover four districts (6.9 percent of the population according to the 1991 Census) for security reasons. These districts reported relatively low levels of mean consumption in the 1992–93 Household Income Survey. These omissions, however, affect only the representativeness of the sample. The analysts adjusted the sample to ensure comparability over time.

WELFARE MEASUREMENT

The welfare indicator commonly chosen was total household expenditure (see table A2). With the exception of urban Ethiopia, Madagascar, and Nigeria, where total expenditures are computed on a per capita basis, all studies used adult equivalence scales to account for household composition. In general, the guiding principle in the selection of items included in each expenditure measure was to ensure comparability over time. Therefore, only items common across surveys and for which questions were asked in a similar fashion were retained. In some cases, such as Zimbabwe, surveys maintained a common design over time, thus allowing for a wide coverage of household consumption expenditures, including use of services, consumption values from assets owned, and imputed values from gifts, remittances, and transfers received. However, there have been instances where this approach led to a more restrictive coverage of household expenditures. For example, in Madagascar, where survey design changed over time, items such as livestock auto-consumption, gifts, remittances, and in-kind payments and auto-consumption from nonfood enterprises were omitted so as to ensure proper comparability. Such items, however, accounted for only 4.3 percent of total expenditure in

1993. The highest number of items omitted is found in Ethiopia (1989–95 rural panel), where only food expenditures were included.

In all cases, consumption included items where imputations were called for. These included imputed rent from owner occupation and imputed income from the consumption of food produced by the household. Methods of computing these imputations differed. Although consumption of own-produced food was included in all expenditure measures, for Ghana the authors used household self-estimation of the value of such items, while in Uganda the imputation was obtained using median unit values from household food purchases (that is, market prices). Such procedures were applied consistently to data sets to preserve comparability over time. Differences across countries, however, would counsel caution in comparing results across countries.

There were also adjustments made to account for differences in prices, across both time and space. All studies computed total expenditures in real terms, where official price series have been used to express values in base year prices (table A2). Moreover, with the exception of Zambia and Zimbabwe, regional and rural-urban price differences are also taken into account in the construction of the consumption measure.

Finally, table A3 provides further details on the computation of the macroeconomic policy scores used in the text.

Table A1. Household Survey Designs

Country/survey years/survey name	Period covered	Sample design	Coverage	Omissions	Sample size: number of households
Ethiopia 1989–97 Rural Panel	Same season across years	Purposively sampled panel	6 villages	See coverage	362
Ethiopia 1994–97 Rural Panel	Same season across years	Purposively sampled panel; two-stage sampling design	15 villages	See coverage	1,403
Ethiopia 1994–97 Urban Panel	Same season across years	Purposively sampled panel	7 major cities	See coverage	1,249
Ghana 1991–92 (GLSS3)	Sep 1991–Sep 1992	Two-stage sampling; stratified	National	None	4,552
Ghana 1998–99 (GLSS4)	Apr 1998–Mar 1999	Same as above	National	None	5,998
Madagascar 1993 (EPM)	May 1993–Apr 1994	Multistage sampling; stratified	National	Islands of Nosy-Bé and Sainte-Marie; about 0.4% of population—census 1993	4,508
Madagascar 1997 (EPM)	Oct 1997–Dec 1997	Same as above	National	Same as above	6,350
Madagascar 1999 (EPM 1999)	Sep 1999–Nov 1999	Same as above	National	Same as above	5,120
Mauritania 1987–88 (LSMS)	Nov 1987–Oct 1988	Two-stage sampling; stratified	National	Nomadic population	1,600
Mauritania 1995–96 (IS)	Oct 1995–June 1996	Same as above	National	Nomadic population	3,450

Survey	Period	Sampling	Coverage	Exclusions	Sample size
Nigeria 1992 (NISH)	Apr 1992–Mar 1993	Two-stage sampling; stratified	National	None	8,955
Nigeria 1996 (NISH)	Apr 1996–Mar 1997	Same as above	National	None	14,381
Uganda 1992–93 (HIS)	Feb 1992–Mar 1993	Multistage sampling; stratified	National	Some rural areas of Kabale district	9,924
Uganda 1996–97 (MS 4)	Feb 1996–Mar 1997	Same as above	National	Kitgum, Kasese, Gulu, and Bundibugy districts; about 6.9% of population—census 1991	6,655
Uganda 1999–2000 (UNHS)	Aug 1999–Sept 2000	Same as above: note panel formed with part of HIS sample	National	Same as above	10,696 (panel: 1,300)
Zambia 1991 (SDAPS)	Oct 1991–Dec 1991	Three-stage sampling; stratified	National	Omission of 15 districts out of 72	9,886
Zambia 1996 (SDAPS)	Oct 1996–Dec 1996	Same as above	National	Omission of 15 districts out of 72	11,770
Zambia 1998 (SDAPS)	Oct 1998–Dec 1998	Same as above	National	None	16,710
Zimbabwe 1990–91 (ICES)	July 1990–June 1991	Two-stage sampling; stratified	National	None	14,264
Zimbabwe 1995–96 (ICES II)	July 1995–June 1996	Same as above	National	None	17,555

Table A2. Welfare Measure Computations

Country and survey years	Welfare measure and price deflation	Main reference
Ethiopia 1989–95	Total food consumption expressed in 1994 prices. Food consumption is deflated by a food price deflator using regional prices collected by the Central Statistical Authority.	Dercon, Stefan. 2002. *The Impact of Economic Reforms on Households in Rural Ethiopia: A Study from 1989 to 1995.* Poverty Dynamics in Africa Series. Washington, D.C.: World Bank.
Ethiopia 1994–97 Rural	Total expenditure expressed in 1994 prices. Expenditure is deflated by a regional consumer price index (CPI) based only on food prices.	Dercon, Stefan. 2000. "Changes in Poverty and Social Indicators in Ethiopia in the 1990s. (At Last) Some Good News from Ethiopia." World Bank, Poverty Reduction and Social Development, Africa Region, Washington, D.C. Processed.
Ethiopia 1994–97 Urban	Total expenditure expressed in 1994 prices. For each site local prices were collected. Expenditure is deflated by using the ratio of each site's poverty line to that of the reference site as deflators.	Dercon, Stefan. 2000. "Changes in Poverty and Social Indicators in Ethiopia in the 1990s. (At Last) Some Good News from Ethiopia." World Bank, Poverty Reduction and Social Development, Africa Region, Washington, D.C. Processed.
Ghana 1991–92 1998–99	Total expenditure expressed in Accra, January 1999 prices. Geographic differences in the cost of living were estimated based on the GLSS4 price questionnaire, and GLSS4 expenditure data used as weights. Based on five localities, Paasche cost of living indexes were constructed for food and nonfood separately. Variations in prices within and between the sample years were allowed for, using the CPI, and using separate series for food and nonfood, as well as for Accra, urban and rural areas.	Coulombe, Harold, and Andrew McKay. 2001. "The Evolution of Poverty and Inequality in Ghana over the 1990s: A Study Based on the Ghana Living Standards Surveys." Office of the Chief Economist, Africa Region, World Bank, May. Processed.
Madagascar 1993 1997 1999	Total expenditure expressed in November 1993, Antananarivo prices. The price data recorded in the 1999 community questionnaire were chosen as the base for calculating regional price indices for 1999 and 1997. For 1993 regional deflation was done based on unit prices calculated from the survey. Temporal deflation was obtained	Paternostro, Stefano, Jean Razafindravonona, and David Stifel. 2001. "Changes in Poverty in Madagascar: 1993–1999." Africa Region Working Paper Series no. 19. Washington, D.C.: World Bank.

56

using Antananarivo price index calculated by the Institut National de la Statistique (INSTAT).

Mauritania

1987

1995

Total expenditure expressed in Nouakchott 1995–96 prices. Temporal deflation was obtained using Nouakchott CPI. Regional deflation was pursued calculating a Laspeyres index, based only on the five items that are available in all four regions and both surveys.

McCulloch, Neil, Bob Baulch, and Milasoa Cherel-Robson. 2000a. "Growth, Inequality and Poverty in Mauritania, 1987–1996." World Bank, Poverty Reduction and Social Development, Africa Region. Washington, D.C. Processed.

Nigeria

1992

1996

Total expenditure expressed in 1996 prices. Adjustment made to account for regional and rural-urban price differences using the CPI of each region.

(a) Nigeria Federal Office of Statistics. 1999. *Poverty Profile for Nigeria: 1980–1996.* Abuja.

(b) Canagarajah, Sudharshan, John Ngwafon, and Foluso Okunmadewa. 2000. "Nigeria's Poverty: Past, Present, and Future." World Bank, Nigeria Country Department, Washington, D.C. Processed.

Uganda

1992–93

1996–97

1999–2000

Total expenditure expressed in 1989 prices. Temporal deflation was done using the composite national CPI. Regional price deflation was obtained using unit values for purchases of major food items to construct regional food price indices for each survey.

Appleton, Simon, Tom Emwanu, Johnson Kagugube, and James Muwonge. 1999. "Changes in Poverty in Uganda, 1992–1997." World Bank, Poverty Reduction and Social Development, Africa Region, Washington, D.C. Processed.

Zambia

1991

1996

1998

Total expenditure expressed in 1991 prices. Temporal deflation was done using the composite national CPI.

McCulloch, Neil, Bob Baulch, and Milasoa Cherel-Robson. 2000b. "Poverty, Inequality and Growth in Zambia during the 1990s." World Bank, Poverty Reduction and Social Development, Africa Region, Washington, D.C. Processed.

Zimbabwe

1990

1995

Total expenditure expressed in 1990 prices. Raw prices for the 23 items used to create the food poverty line were collected from the Central Statistical Office. An index was created using the food poverty line weights. The ratio of such index to a base value was used as deflator. Variability over time and province was ensured. No adjustment was possible for urban-rural differentials.

Alwang, Jeffrey, Bradford Mills, and Nelson Taruvinga. 1999. "Changes in Well-Being in Zimbabwe, 1990–1996: Non-Parametric Evidence." World Bank, Poverty Reduction and Social Development, Africa Region, Washington, D.C. Processed.

Table A3. Computations of Macroeconomic Policy Scores

Country	Period of change	Fiscal policy						Monetary policy						Exchange rate policy						Overall macroeconomic policy	Weighted[d]
		Change in overall fiscal balance excluding all grants (% of GDP)		Change in total government revenue (% of GDP)		Change in fiscal policy	Change in seigniorage		Change in inflation		Change in monetary policy	Change in real effective exchange rate		Change in black market premium		Change in exchange rate policy	Average score	average score
		% points	Score	% points	Score	Score[a]	% points	Score	% points	Score	Score[b]	% points	Score	% points	Score	Score[c]		
Côte d'Ivoire	1985–88	-11.6	-2	-5.2	-1	-3.0	-2.7	2	2.9	0	1.0	21.8	-2	-2.1	0	-1.0	-1.0	-1.5
Ethiopia	1989–95	0.3	0.0	-6.9	-1	-1.0	-0.7	1	2.9	0	0.5	-55.8	3	-56.0	2	2.5	0.7	1.0
	1994–97	2.5	1	6.1	1	2.0	-3.8	2	-6.8	1	1.5	-23.9	2	-126.6	3	2.5	2.0	2.2
Ghana	1988–92	-2.3	-1	0.1	0	-1.0	-1.2	1	-10.1	2	1.5	-23.5	2	-51.0	2	2	0.8	0.8
	1992–98	-5.0	-1	4.5	1	0.0	0.4	0	7.9	-1	-0.5	-11.9	1	-4.4	0	0.5	0.0	0.2
Madagascar	1993–97	0.8	0	-0.5	0	0.0	-1.1	1	13.7	-2	-0.5	-0.2	0	-8.0	0	0.0	-0.2	-0.1
	1997–99	1.7	1	1.6	0	1.0	-0.2	0	-16.8	2	1.0	2.3	0	1.4	0	0.0	0.7	0.5
Mauritania	1987–95	9.2	3	0.6	0	3.0	-1.3	1	-1.1	0	0.5	-35.8	3	-84.2	2	2.5	2.0	2.4
Nigeria	1985–92	0.4	0	12.3	1	1.0	1.0	-1	-1.8	0	-0.5	-518.9	3	-260.4	3	3.0	1.2	1.9
	1992–96	3.7	2	-4.6	-1	1.0	-1.2	1	31.4	-3	-1.0	53.3	-2	249.1	-3	-2.5	-0.8	-1.0
Uganda	1992–97	2.9	1	3.3	1	2.0	-1.8	1	-30.3	2	1.5	10.2	-2	-23.0	1	-0.5	1.0	0.7
	1997–00	-0.5	0	0.3	0	0.0	0.4	0	-4.5	1	0.5	-8.9	1	-5.8	0	0.5	0.3	0.3
Zambia	1991–96	1.7	1.0	1.0	0	1.0	-2.7	2	-63.2	2	2.0	-8.4	1	-350.7	3	2.0	1.7	1.6
	1996–98	2.2	1	-0.7	0	1.0	-0.9	1	-9.2	1	1.0	11.0	-2	1.7	0	-1	0.3	0.0
Zimbabwe	1991–96	-2.6	-1	-0.8	0	-1.0	1.6	-1	4.2	0	-0.5	-8.0	1	-40.6	2	1.5	0.0	0.3

Table A3. (continued)

Country	Period of change	Fiscal policy — Change in overall fiscal balance excluding all grants (% of GDP) % points	Score	Fiscal policy — Change in total government revenue (% of GDP) % points	Score	Change in fiscal policy Score[a]	Monetary policy — Change in seigniorage % points	Score	Monetary policy — Change in inflation % points	Score	Change in monetary policy Score[b]	Exchange rate policy — Change in real effective exchange rate % points	Score	Exchange rate policy — Change in black market premium % points	Score	Change in exchange rate policy Score[c]	Overall macroeconomic policy Average score	Weighted[d] average score
Scoring criteria[e]																		
	−3	≤ −5.0							≥ 31.0					≥51.0				
	−2	−4.9 to −2.0		≤ −4.0			2.0 to 3.9		10 to 30.9			≥10.0		16 to 50				
	−1	−1.9 to 0.9					1.0 to 1.9		5.0 to 9.9			5.0 to 9.9		5.0 to 15				
	0			−3.9 to 3.0		n.a.	−0.5 to 0.9		−2.4 to 4.9		n.a.	−2.0 to 4.9		−9.0 to 4.0		n.a.	n.a.	n.a.
	1	1.0 to 2.9		≥ 3.1			−2.0 to −0.6		−9.9 to −2.5			−2.1 to −14.9		−29 to −10				
	2	3.0 to 4.9					−3.0 to −2.1		−49.0 to −10.0			−15.0 to −30.9		−99 to −30				
	3	≥ 5.0										≤ −31.0		≤ −100				

n.a. Not applicable.
a. Sum of scores for change in overall fiscal balance and change in revenue.
b. Average of scores for change in seigniorage and change in inflation.
c. Average of scores for change in the real effective exchange rate and change in the black market premium.
d. Weights derived from cross-sectional growth regressions.
e. As used in World Bank 1994.
Source: World Bank 1994; authors' computations from World Bank data.

Notes

1. In support of this hypothesis, Guillaumont, Guillaumont, and Brun (1999) find that economic, political, and natural volatilities are important factors in explaining the poor growth performance of African economies.

2. A "spell" is a period between two household surveys.

3. This is based on the growth in mean household income or consumption. If growth is taken to be per capita private consumption from the national accounts, the elasticity is approximately –2.

4. Using more recent and more comparable data, Knowles (2001) finds significant negative effects of inequality on growth.

5. According to Ravallion (2001, p. 1810), a country with high inequality (with a Gini coefficient of, say, 60 percent) would be expected to have a growth elasticity of poverty of –1.2. If the initial Gini coefficient were only 30 percent, the elasticity would be –2.1.

6. The selection of countries was based on the availability of comparable measures of consumption, and includes Ethiopia, Ghana, Madagascar, Mauritania, Nigeria, Uganda, Zambia, and Zimbabwe. The book also draws on an analysis of time series data from the Demographic and Health Surveys. References to these Poverty Dynamics studies are given in the bibliography.

7. Recall that the Gini ratio varies from 0 (perfect income equality) to 1 (perfect inequality). The higher the value, the greater the inequality.

8. Although most welfare measures are based on expenditures, we use the terms "income" and "consumption" interchangeably. For most countries, expenditure is normalized on the number of "equivalent" adults in the household. In urban Ethiopia, Nigeria, and Madagascar, the welfare measure is real household expenditure *per capita*. Another exception is rural Ethiopia

(1989–95), where the welfare measure used is real household food consumption expenditure.

9. Intuitively, the Gini index of a population represents the expected income difference between two randomly selected individuals or households. From table 1 we know that in Zimbabwe real average per capita consumption in 1996 amounted to US$439. The corresponding Gini index is 0.64 (table 5). Thus, in 1996 the per capita consumption of any two randomly selected Zimbabweans differed on average by US$281 (= 0.64*US$439)—a clear indication of high inequality, given that average per capita consumption is only US$439.

10. This is defined as the proportionate change in headcount poverty divided by the proportionate change in mean per capita household expenditure. For details of the method used, see Kakwani and Pernia (2000).

11. The tendency for income inequality to narrow as higher-income groups bear the brunt of economic recession was also noted by Grootaert (1996) in analyzing poverty changes in Côte d'Ivoire in the 1980s, although this does not seem to have occurred in Zambia during 1991–96.

12. When mean household expenditures are declining, $\phi = \eta_g/\eta$, so that a recession would also be considered pro-poor if $\phi > 1$.

13. This is simply the slope coefficient in the regression of the proportionate change in headcount poverty on the proportionate change in the survey mean. The standard error on the slope coefficient is 0.18. Note that the regression line in figure 1 runs almost through the origin, a reflection of the fact that income inequality has been stable over this period. The historical elasticity we observe for this sample of African countries is significantly lower than that estimated by Ravallion (2001) to be typical of low-income countries (–2.5). Given the different poverty lines used (he uses the much lower benchmark of PPP US$1/day) and the different method of computation, his estimates are not comparable with ours.

14. The data used in many previous assessments were often of doubtful quality and, given the lags involved in implementing the reforms, the 1990s might be a more appropriate decade to examine the growth path induced by economic policy reforms in Africa (Collier and Gunning 1999, p. 101).

15. Ali (1998) gets quite different results, with reforms being associated with increasing poverty. This is probably because of the different poverty data sets he uses (derived from IFAD data). Our concern here has been to use only data where careful attention has been paid to comparability over time. Without further information about Ali's data, it is difficult to establish the specific reasons for the differences in results.

16. Both poverty changes and macroeconomic policy scores might be favorably affected by a third factor—movements in the terms of trade, for example.

17. Although we track and compare three-year averages of the macropolicy stance, we do so only for the two periods prescribed by the available household surveys.

18. These countries are described by Collier and Gunning (1999, p. 102) as "providing at least modest levels of social order, macroeconomic order and resource allocation."

19. The different components of the ICRG political risk index (maximum scores in brackets) are government stability (12), socioeconomic conditions (12), investment profile (12), internal conflict (12), external conflict (12), corruption (12), military in politics (6), religion in politics (6), law and order (6), ethnic tensions (6), democratic accountability (6), and bureaucracy quality (4). The maximum score is 100. A political risk score below 49.9 indicates very high risk; a score between 50 and 59.9, high risk; 60 to 69.9, moderate risk; 70 to 79.9, low risk; and 80 or more, very low risk. Similarly, a score of 49.9 percent or below on an individual risk component would imply that the component can be considered very high risk, a score in the 50 to 59.9 percent range, high risk, and so on. For a detailed description of the ICRG rating system, we refer to http://www.icrgonline.com/icrgMethods.asp.

20. In all, 13 episodes of institutional change were examined. Political risk scores for our survey periods were not available for Mauritania and Côte d'Ivoire.

21. Using two-year averages of the survey year and the year prior to the survey year to account for lags in the effect of institutional change on poverty does not change the results. Our findings are also robust to the use of a subset of the political risk indicator focusing on indicators of political stability (government stability, internal conflict, and external conflict) and governance (corruption, law and order, democratic accountability, and bureaucratic quality).

22. Because the study is not nationally representative, the results cannot be generalized to Ethiopia as a whole. Nonetheless, the methodology used and the empirical findings provide important insights in the linkages between economic policy, growth, and poverty reduction.

23. These reflect mainly changes in food crop prices. Coffee prices also improved, yet it was grown in only one of the six sampled villages, and the coffee harvest had failed that year in that particular village because of a pest attack and drought. The effect of changing export crop prices cannot be evaluated from this sample, but its importance has been assessed explicitly in the Uganda case study described on p. 34.

24. Dercon (1995) shows that the cereal marketing margins improved mainly because of the liberalization of the grain markets, and only on some routes did the end of the war have a significant effect.

25. Adult education levels are extremely low—less than one year per adult—and they are assumed not to have changed. The effect of education as such, as

opposed to changes in returns to education, has thus not been evaluated in this study.

26. Because the direct effect of changing producer prices has been controlled for, changes in returns to land result from other factors, such as shifts in the underlying production technology potentially induced by the reforms.

27. This finding was confirmed by the repeated cross-sectional multivariate analysis (Coulombe and McKay 2001).

28. One constraint these studies face is the absence of reliable price data (linked, that is, to the household data), which would be needed to assess the direct impact of the reforms on consumption. Systematic changes in real producer prices are certain to have affected income distribution and poverty during this period. However, both the Madagascar and Zimbabwe studies control for rainfall shocks, an issue to which we return on p. 43.

Bibliography

The word *processed* describes informally reproduced works that may not be commonly available through libraries. Studies completed under the Poverty Dynamics in Africa Initiative are noted with the symbol §.

Abdulai, Awudu. 2000. "Spatial Price Transmission and Asymmetry in the Ghanaian Maize Market." *Journal of Development Economics* 63(2): 327–49.

Abdulai, Awudu, and Christopher Delgado. 2000. "An Empirical Investigation of Short- and Long-Run Agricultural Wage Formation in Ghana." *Oxford Development Studies* 28(2):169–85.

Alesina, Alberto, and Roberto Perotti. 1994. "The Political Economy of Growth: A Critical Survey of the Recent Literature." *World Bank Economic Review* 8(3):351–71.

Ali, A. A. G. 1998. "Structural Adjustment and Poverty in Sub-Saharan Africa: 1985–1995." In Thandika Mkandawire and Charles C. Soludo, eds., *African Perspectives on Structural Adjustment, Vol. 2.* International Development Research Centre, Ottawa, Canada.

§Alwang, Jeffrey. 2000. "Structural Adjustment, Drought, and Poverty in Zimbabwe. Changes in the 1990s." World Bank, Poverty Reduction and Social Development, Africa Region, Washington, D.C. Processed.

§Alwang, Jeffrey, and Lire Ersado. 1999. "Changes in Poverty in Zimbabwe: 1990–1996." World Bank, Poverty Reduction and Social Development, Africa Region, Washington, D.C. Processed.

§Alwang, Jeffrey, Bradford Mills, and Nelson Taruvinga. 1999. "Changes in Well-Being in Zimbabwe, 1990–1996: Non-Parametric Evidence." World Bank, Poverty Reduction and Social Development, Africa Region, Washington, D.C. Processed.

§———. 2002. *Why Has Poverty Increased in Zimbabwe?*" Poverty Dynamics in Africa Series. Washington, D.C.: World Bank.

§Appleton, Simon. 2001. "Poverty in Uganda, 1999/2000: Preliminary Estimates from the Uganda National Household Survey." University of Nottingham, United Kingdom, January. Processed.

§Appleton, Simon, Tom Emwanu, Johnson Kagugube, and James Muwonge. 1999. "Changes in Poverty in Uganda, 1992–1997." World Bank, Poverty Reduction and Social Development, Africa Region, Washington, D.C. Processed.

Aron, Janine. 2000. "Growth and Institutions: A Review of the Evidence." *World Bank Research Observer* 15(1):99–135.

Badiane, O., and G. Shively. 1998. "Spatial Integration, Transport Costs, and the Response of Local Prices to Policy Changes in Ghana." *Journal of Development Economics* 56(2):411–31.

Bourguignon, François. 2000. "Can Redistribution Accelerate Growth and Development?" Paper presented at the World Bank ABCDE/Europe Conference, Paris, June 26–28.

Bourguignon, François, and Christian Morrisson. 1992. *Adjustment and Equity in Developing Countries: A New Approach.* Paris: OECD Development Centre.

Bouton, Lawrence, Christine Jones, and Miguel Kiguel. 1994. *Macroeconomic Reform in Africa: "Adjustment in Africa" Revisited.* Policy Research Working Paper no. 1394. Washington, D.C.: World Bank.

Brock, William A., and Steven N. Durlauf. 2000. *Growth Economics and Reality.* National Bureau of Economic Research Working Paper Series, no. 8041:1–48, December.

§Canagarajah, Sudharshan, John Ngwafon, and Foluso Okunmadewa. 2000. "Nigeria's Poverty: Past, Present, and Future." World Bank, Nigeria Country Department, Washington, D.C. Processed.